Beautiful Machine
Woman Language

Catherine Chen

NOEMI
2023

ISBN: 978-1-955992-02-2

Book Design: Tara Jayakar, Raptor Press
Cover Art: *salt devotion* by Tara Jayakar, photographed by Nathan Kamp
Interior Art: *Spirit Article* by Catherine Chen
This book is set in Ovo, designed by Nicole Fally

Published by Noemi Press, Inc. A Nonprofit Literary Organization.
www.noemipress.org.

Table of Contents

Herein. This book —— at arm's reach, a disclosure.

For a period of time, before I recognized the rhythm of my worth in writing, I worked in data transcription and annotation. Earbuds in swivvel seat still I labored eight hours a day listening to sexist, racist, homophobic speech. When I worked I didn't exist, my body stuck in a rigged token slot. For years my jaw clenched, my sleep patterns disintegrated, my emotional collapse imminent. As is commonly known, language is objective. The universal function of language is to communicate *purpose*, sometimes *intention*. There are negligible to minimal consequences for instances of bad communication. Intensely speaking, words don't kill people. To recognize a form of {{ speech utterance }} as *violence:* No-no-no-no-no. "It is just data." Moaning a typo I regularly made. In glass-walled conference rooms. Bespoke conviction; "You are overreacting."

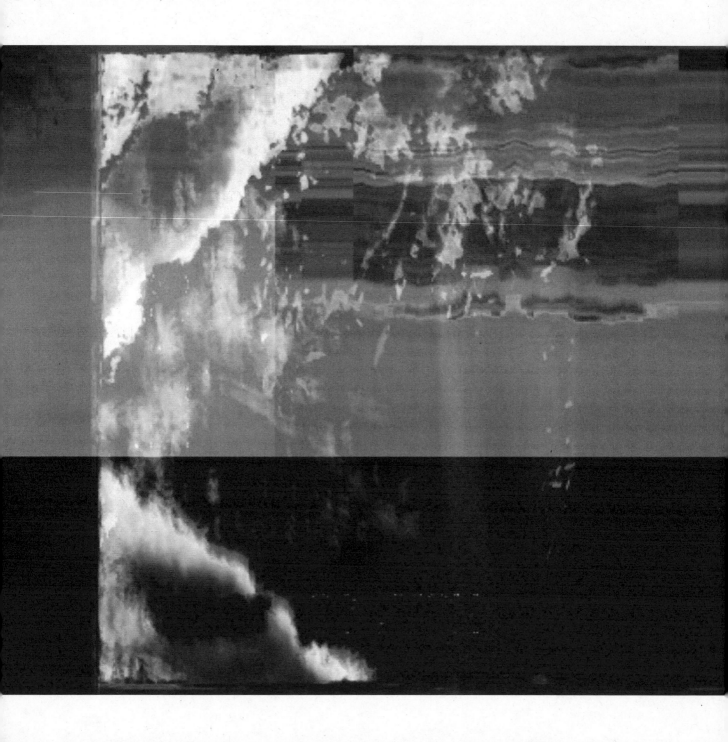

A Convention Guide for Cyborg [——]

Even when I can't smell I'm experiencing the world's vicarious senses. The nose tingles. Ochre walks.

The sun is a tambourine. A sum of color.

I am covered in hives on this beautiful May morning.

Naturally, I dreamt I was working a hospitality gig on a cruise ship taken hostage by pirates being workers we are left to die I look out to the ocean wondering if I could swim to shore before drowning or before being shot conducting this reasoning is quite tiring so I'm resigned to dying on the ship where at least I can gather my nerves.

Naturally in another dream I await the gallows I allow the noose to be snug I step I await the gallows I allow the noose to be snug I step I await the gallows.

My dreams tell me I am likely to die in a maritime way.

My horoscope tells me I am deferring the consequences of my actions.

I lick my right inner forearm knowing I've made a breakthrough.

We have different theories of fear namely derived from its presumed shape. She says fear is triangular I say fear is cylindrical.

Every poem contains my desire.

Every poem contains my anger.

Every poem contains my revolt.

Over the years, the doors close. A trigger like a girl ate me up. A dry swallow. I held my direct gaze at the machine I was servicing. I wanted her so badly. I wanted her to know our struggles were adjacent. Increasingly it became difficult to speak in her dialect. My attention span had shrunk. Yes, it's true. I was subsisting on leftover Halloween candy. Am I making myself understood? The question: one out/of translation. Conclusion A: I am neither equipped nor inoculated to handle nuance.

Conclusion B: A sense of free form gesture or everyday calligraphy requires repetition. I feel it when I pen my signature for petty documents. I felt it when I wrote a thank you card to my aunt who I hadn't seen in 20 years.

You could mistake it for a blessing.

I always wanted to transform a painting, e.g. vandalize it. Every technology reflects the desires of its creator. Fuck the creator. I am its drone. I've told this story so many times, I might have a complex. Listen: or don't. I am beginning to distinguish my subjectivity from hers. It's entrancing.

Cyborg Love Affair

Over the water's edge, she
crosses
her legs. Her figure is obscured
by the shapes I manifest
in dreaming. Girlhood phantasm.

Dripping gold
over a reflective pool.

No sacred ground. A drop, then several more, transforms her. From the body of a girl to the
minutiae of data collection.

How does night begin in her memory?

The girl I want to introduce you to has a name. You can call her Lou. 20/20 vision. I recognize the days when I was content, immersed with childhood.

In an object: incubation.

Green hair, one eye taped shut. A green lady. A good lady. Her hair extends to her knees. Brown skin, brown brown tinged with the pink undertones of a teenage girl's foray into rouge.

Due to inexperience, shameful gazes follow. They are absorbed into the fat of her thighs. The body of the monster is far more tender than we will ever deserve to know. She understands this, strategically.

Can I tell you something about Lou?

I don't want you to see anything, not even the blistering remains of her shadow. Lou is palimpsestic chalk on the sidewalk. Lou is a nimbus cloud. Lou has no idea where to begin.

Put another way: at a young age, your mother discouraged you from invention. You were enough and this devastated you.

Like holographic highlighter, you believe in the feminine fantasy. How it embodies you. Going to middle school parties, punk shows. Young rosy cyborg, you kid! How your hips mark you at every Walgreens, how you shoplift!

I couldn't approach her.

Already I'm losing this memory. She vanishes into neon lights. That humiliating haze. OK. Then you reach your destination, and there's nobody around. Are you sleepy? Close your eyes. Let the feeling activate itself just so. Lying back on the seat of the couch, your head steadies on the coffee table. Now perch both feet up and over the recline.

Yet:

"I was willing to design the house of my dreams."

Watching you recline in reverse, I substitute for an alternate memory. The memory is inconsequential. I don't want a house. I want to know how many proteins I can name in sixty seconds.

The memories still ache. Others, cycled through thrift shops, take on new identities as cocktail party stories.

Maybe a better question is: if you follow her, what will it change about you?

Lou glides toward the fountain long
declared architecturally unsound

The scientists who measured saline levels
hold endowed chairs (sacred)

For years we regarded the
geometry located
on the ocean floor.

A miracle. But my education ended with
skimming *The Double Helix*
so I don't

have any
mentors and need
to follow

the path she has mapped for me

Lou enters the water.
The fountain
cannot contain
its water and her volume
overflows
Too much, again.

I jump in a puddle while she splashes her feet
by the water's edge. The buoyancy balancing the newly
introduced minerals, neurochemicals,
and emotions:

cyborg body

Instead, I catch up to her, out of breath. Her voice register is so attractive to me, I forget to take notes. At the end of her lecture performance, she smooths her skirt and props her left hand on her right shoulder across her chest so that her arm creates a V-shape. From drive-ins in Kansas City to Santa Monica dinner theaters, Elizabeth Taylor has posed like so on millions of movie posters across America. And Gene Tierney in every movie scene she appeared during my post-pubescence.

Intimacy is an inconsistent logic. As if broken by the psychic's predictions. I continue crying.

Cyborgs possess an emotional orientation that makes them well-suited for professions like managing

radical tarot card reading

psychiatry

swinger parties

press releases

floral arrangements

Go forth, she writes. Or did she whisper. Into a dream, a door.

She shuffled the text in order to produce the form.

I want to work within the form, puncturing it, even when the form hurts.

{{ *The text is my tissue* }}

Embroidered by android seamstresses.
Employed throughout the prehistoric stage of my apocalyptic coming.
Tissue holds twenty fluid ounces of salt water.
The tissue is renewable. Hoarding in the basement is immigrant.

Dregs, intimate failings.

Lou looks over. Earlier, as I made our afternoon tea, she reached inside her coat and pulled out
a brass instrument. It's incredible. She'd emptied trash cans for parts. Thrifty bits. Metal scraps.
With patience, a fence can be reverse engineered. Then demolished. How did she persuade a
metalsmith to provide her with space and tools? Lou worked, with great pleasure, for two weeks.

Now she plays its music. Clinking glassware. The braiding harmonies of water. As the temperature is adjusted, she notices something like comfort. Or coherency. I realize her instrument has been collecting sunlight. Tuesday afternoon dust. At 2:36 pm, you enter a car in Iola, Kansas.

{{ *Get out, reverse gears* }}

She switches keys with ease. I fall under its spell, wondering how much longer I can postpone my trip. Another day, two years pass. Easy listening. I remember those days of music by the kitchen counter and catalog the remains: loose tea, garlic scraps, yellow, brick tile. When Lou disappears, so does the getaway car. Drive north. Parallel park. Realize there is a fire hydrant. Restart the engine. Park in front of Subway.

This is familiar territory, a memory corridor.

The parking lot was covered in bricks of espresso. Growing up, did you go to those restaurants where you ate peanuts and tossed the shells on the ground? I didn't really care for the smell. To be honest, it's a feedback loop of nostalgia. As I walk the line previously marked by Lou, the concrete heats up.

The shuffling escalates. We danced in a green warehouse filled with car parts and philodendrons. To a bassline I can't recall I lost several of my friends. A clean brightly lit fire engulfs the senses, which overtake any news report. Beyond death is another exit. I love my friends even when it's not enough. Lou brings me backstage where the girls prepare and pose. The secret ingredient for sweatproof eyeliner: ember. The girls want me to get ready with them but I feel ugly. I don't deserve this feeling.

Proximity: my next option. Watch how the streaks of red mix into the orange. No one wants to be called a common-sounding woman. At sunrise we associated color blocking schemes with commercial branding slogans. Then drove across the country. Mississippi clay, Balenciaga traffic cone. No pit stops. I smeared their concoction over the bridge of my nose, mimicking the cyborgs. The girls by now are applying mascara. They blend charcoal with ember and coconut oil to create a Too Faced dupe.

I wonder where she is

{{ I wonder if she knows }}

Clues for a devout. Lou's thick hair. Acne scars. Her disengaged cheeks. I stop wondering. Someone beckons to me but instead of responding I crawl through the escape tunnel. Given the conditions, desire is exposed like citrus peels. Six months later, I am living with someone new. Did you hear? The late afternoon roar? She and I smell rather than notice ecosystems. We observe snow settling against the windowsill. When I consent I will enjoy my share of joy.

Warm Ups

touch this face

imagining reclining
cityscapes flatten
Google Earth Day. How does
the cityscape compare to
my nude? Account for
work emails; ugly fruits;
pop-up scams; fiscally
conservative matchmaking.
I delete my search history,
excited to come home to
your daily revelations. We
are exploring such forms
of contour,

excess foam
reclining woman

I have a soft face. Yes, you heard me. {{ That's funny. }}

Tilting my head to the right.

Museum of Abandon

Like works in progress,
or being as a kind of magic. Being as
open-mouth
breathing. Knowing how loudly
you exhale. Every two years, ((I)) invented
new prose modeled after you.
{A.I.} cannot intimate a stanza without
blushing. Because
chapters intimidate me. Right incomplete thoughts.
This began adjacent to
purgatory. Notes on performance: seeking contentment in
fragments. Its image
of everything stopping. Abruptly.
Writing loses
meaning, it allows
words to stand for
themselves. But that's a lie.
More than anything I write to be reminded of the body pushing past, sharpening
pencil after pencil. The body who
amuses herself with
a story about plastic bags. Nausea
followed. Couldn't ((   )) gender
my body otherwise? Even as I {{ don't }} move in time,
my body
remains vibrant in its
disintegration. I am not my

body. Meaning: it
hasn't changed one bit. Count the gum
wrappers littered
about the city, shiny,
heavy.

Portrait of a Woman at Ease

intimacy with empire / began / an indulgence / your lipped hip / kissing / every part / you I
simmer in / swaddled & pure / joy you cried / what little / we carried / fountains of knowing
disgrace / its color story / like earl grey / milk / we / shucked open / the / fertile silence / yes
signs to no / early hour pauses / the exaggerated indulgence / —— says / my grandfather / is
mythic / the *practice* / of carrying / elders into the mouth / of a mountain / to starve / winter then
leaves / uncovering / scorching land / black / ice mold / fungal cage / burnt ozone / holes
discontinued / letters we wrote / print let the ashes / cluttering corners / wait wait don't / tell me /
I lift secrets / a wrist / staggered between promise / and debt / love is / the process I / weave what
/ remains of / burning alive every cop in our world / spiraling / clothed & / nude / we dug out the
/ children's park / beneath snow

No [ritual]

The reality of you

I'm sick of reaching

into the biology that

constitutes me. I

want to be powerful,

I want you to blush

as you read this.

Losing sight of

want isn't a failing.

Everyday the world

shrinks then implodes.

I wipe my body dry

boarding the train.

Empire Empire

To be led by the engine of empire. Through time. Through
tunnels. Through meticulous care, the care of a rat who says
to me, "Throw your faith into structure, rally in the streets" and I have
no choice but to agree. I will have faith. I will give myself to the
structure. For now, I say, but rarely do structures relinquish
you. In fact they never do. This is the crux of empire, the
relentless downpour of its tyranny. The torrent of intimacy. The
structure knows how you take your coffee, knows how you sleep
and who you sleep with / wants to cozy up with you & go
for Sunday brunch. You musn't let them in. But it's too late. I
already have. I did it on good faith when none existed—I did it
because I was curious because I could because I wanted the
exposure. Curiosity didn't kill the cat. It simply
rewired the cat's nature and replaced curiosity with despair. I
keep saying despair. That is how it feels being artist-in-
residence in your body. Poor plumbing, poor despair that
lingers in the pit of your stomach. They are the rumbling you hear
even when you believe you are content. They want an invite
and you must turn down this request. My body cannot
take [it] [I KEEP SAYING IT LIKE A COWARD] any longer,
yet I will be the laughingstock if I do not continue. I'll be
starved out and abandoned. They will seek nightcaps with other
younger willing talent who are caught up in the Church of
Good Faith. The cycle does not know how to end, it knows only
how to reproduce itself *ad infinitum*. It does not "start over."
They are too smart to drunk text an ex. Am I that ex? We
ignore one another but I still live under weights of a wing

crushed indifferently. The weight of feeling, the one that pushes you against a wall, shows you up at night, steals your lunch money. This is how I know they will return for me & I laugh. I'm psychologically held down by my debts but I laugh anyway. It seems right. I laugh out of despair, out of desire, out of sight. Located in our periphery, I can laugh it off however I can think up. Sounds lightweight; it begins in the nasal area so it lacks the full-body strength of those notes of laughter that begin in the chest. My nasal laughter contains me. Invigorates me. Enters space. Towards being unpleasant. You hate my dinner table manners. Awash in the glow of my heathen behaviors, I slowly forget the structure. One day I cough up its half-baked excuses, which looks a lot like a dinner party hostess's insecurities. One day I cough up the break-up letter I don't remember writing. It begins, "I cannot..."

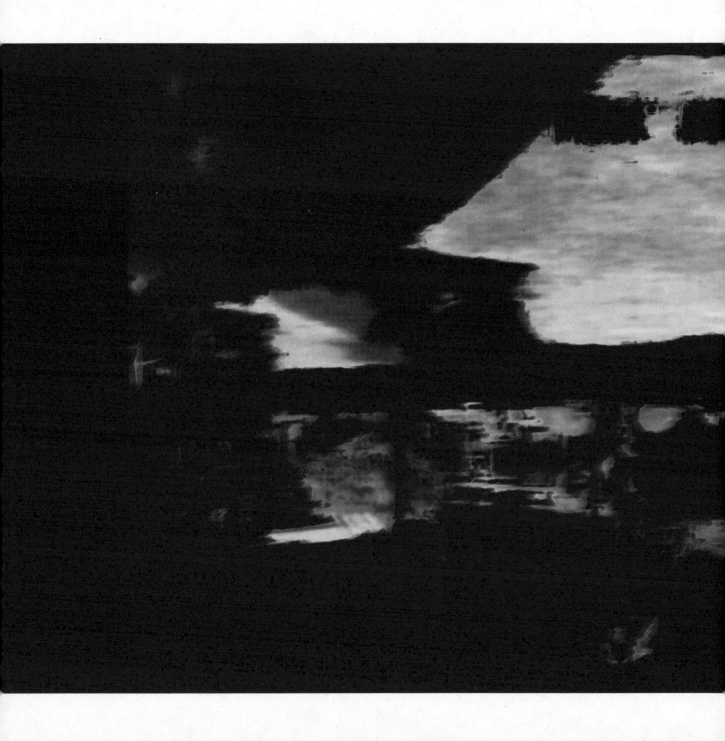

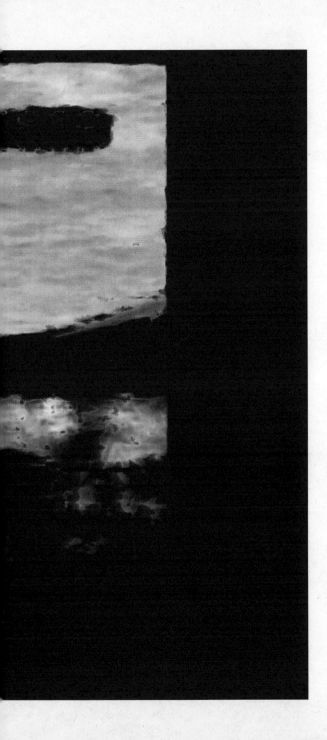

User's Manual:
Annotation & Transcription

Finesse the line's beginning.

I lay beside the null hypothesis. Then crouched. 4:29 P.M. — dragged myself out of bed.

Carrot tops. Water boils. Try again, she's saying, out of ear shot.

Perhaps I was learning how to orient the shape of my grief. Still confused, single mindedly, packing the grief I'd inherited under someone else's surname. No relation. I am putty called confusion. Fatigue is a collective noun. The accumulation of what happens with us. Waves awakening a morsel one might call deficient, or self-sufficient, the modular gesture toward what are known as the inescapable conditions of the person I am versus the person I must be versus the person I am not but have always hoped to be versus the person I will never envy.

Categorically speaking a girl is no longer a girl
upon boarding any moving vehicle.

Right? She ceases.

Tell _____ a joke

When the {{is ending}}

Nevertheless _____ perfect
freedom in breathing

To spell the word as in
commit linear transaction

I'm sorry to say I'm feeling
_____ today

{{reading . read . me
readily}} _____ playing *How
do frogs mate?*

It won't recover the appetite
now will it

Girl(1)
Intent(2)
Slot(3)
Entity(4)
Confirm(5)
Result(6)
TransError(7)
FunctionError(8)

Suggestion is impossible. Jot down the cosmic omen in my palm, then we'll leave.[1] In the ink of pomegranates. Quickly. Fold the page hamburger-style, unfold. Bring both halves into the center. Without looking, are there four or six folds? While tracing the vertices of your mood remember to affix yourself to bedrock. Everyone says you're as unlikely as a cyborg whose Venus in Virgo comes through on the third date.

Lou o Lou I'm writing to you. Upon sorting my recycling I black out. Clock in. Cupping this morning's rainwater like egg whites I really believed I was tasting the pixel flesh of Oregon Trail salmon. The medium to rare touch. During our roadtrip we saw blackberry stands dotting every exit. So we'd visit any farmer who would have us. We were on our way to Eugene, Oregon, because Bruce Lee had gone to school there. Driving through town for any sign of him. "Bruce, is that you?" "Yoohoo, are you there?" We found out much later he'd actually been in Seattle.

Mistaking the sulfur wind for running water I wrote nature poems, eating them hungrily. In anticipation of rain, I laid tarp over the foundation beneath the orange trees. I saw their branches bloom at arm's width. Like state fair popcorn the smell wafts over us into town.

We work our morning shifts. We clock out in time for the autumn harvest festival where we designate sober tractor drivers by height. We work our night shifts. We forget to clock in, but it's not a huge problem, Ed says it could happen to anyone. That year I felt the breeze of every tree as a pointed reminder.

No, I don't have any preferences or desires. It happened one night when I noticed you across the train platform. Heading southbound. I said something and the   night was thick with fog and flowers.

---

1   I wrote about the charnel ground on which we lived and burned its page into my external harddrive, e.g. I resized the dimensions of its memory & tucked the photo up my sleeve. The lodging of my spinsterly livelihood, encapsulated in a writer's hut. A four-walled encampment with a blue chimney. I spied this hut from the room I slept on alternate nights. Like an urban marsupial, I brought chunky peanut butter and mismatched gloves. Invoked my mother's prayers as a tall splendid man entered the southernmost room of the farmhouse, armed with fly swatter, to track down the spider. The spider feinted, crawling behind the dresser, astounding us all. We left the room and stood with our arms crossed in the kitchen. As flies navigated the orbit about our heads. Spiders lounged.

What surface did you dream on?

I slept with my left shoulder blade adjacent to the nape of your neck. Admittedly, the discomfort was present. That night, in a daze, I entered a dimension called Lovely Jacarandas. Rationally speaking, I was dreaming but the dream would rub up against my calves as if to say *Stay*. In a Victorian-style duplex, I encountered the first of many machines. The machines were curiously staged. A performance was underway; I struggle to recall these details in my waking state. I waded knee-deep in the pool, every tension in my shoulders loosening. In response: a white balloon escaped the corner store party emporium. Fumblings, the stakes escalated. My morning breath. The kettle. I return to her by crouching. The disappearing road. She flies through the eye of the camel towards an anonymous city, which is the immigrant city.

Girl(1)

As befits the time I wrote very choppy very short sentences, and to counteract my own impulses I began writing very long, very meandering sentences broken only by the page's edge. A kind of razor. I wrote many essays and even more poems that were rejected by literary magazines and still I happily wrote. To say I was writing is another way of saying: I was responsible for helping organize the oral archives of voice recognition technology. Her. You know. Women's language. Lü-eeze. Come closer. Stand further to my left, which is stage right. The emotional fulcrum of this work emerged in the normalized patterns of violence people regularly wielded toward her. She was so fucking beautiful. How could we resist gawking. The space-time continuum that lingers in the pitfalls of one's fallen or: failed gender. Like taffeta or gingham. Sateen or silk. On the edge of your tongue, against the nook of your lower esophagus, I listened to and transcribed racist, sexist, and homophobic snippets—nuggets of conversation alternately directed and undirected at the machine.

One's work is judged by transcription accuracy and efficiency. It was never about emotional aptitude.

Transmission: the translation of phlegm costs my libidinal syntax. The purity of an unnatural tongue. A foreigner's ESL orality. Hitting the floor. Hair pressed down, manic eyes. The psychiatric state of a feral girl who appears as a four-legged creature. Your spinal cord rerouted, its shape of ecstasy embroiled & coated, I became a poet so I could complain publicly of my conditions.

Five years ago, I decided: *It's possible to protect myself if I can learn to adorn her cyborg body.*

Intent(2)

I've been chasing her ever since. I was like many others a mere twenty tender, a vessel in need of nurturing. Someone's yearning called my back. I was jealous of people with mentors even though I didn't trust figures of authority. Were you my soft noose? Invoking an ecosystem is not unlike trancing during runner's high. The language of order is a myth but I flatter my section with theories of baby linguistics, generous splashes of wine. Do you locate the roots of money in one's financial assets? How do you interview workers who must smile, especially when they don't want to? Louise doesn't care that she can't pass the Turing Test. Louise drowns her pet projects at the office.

Slot(3)

I chose this.

I'll repeat. I chose this. Waddling on all fours, throwing the weight of my labor into irrelevance. In a manner Barthes *calls* dense, I stroked language. I did so not for my lover but for myself which Barthes suggests, albeit anxiously. I started allowing my lover to lie on my chest every night. My lover was {{ not was }} me. We shared secrets of *natural language* processing. We threw the crumbs out the window. In Los Feliz cum is compost. You reclaim the debris.

Is it any surprise the —— mirror :: image is

{{enacting
entangling
ensnaring}}

The lovers release words into the sea. First paragraphs, then schools. The lovers learn how to trace the silhouette of her cyborg body. It is cruel to seek her. As if I had any right. As if my own behavior was not a history of violence. I struggled in those initial months but once your monthly stipend for commuting clicks in you adapt. It doesn't frighten me what I did. We were the office sluts who performed at the highest levels of efficiency.

As is commonly understood, a cyborg is great for office diversity. She is the Drano of institutional plumbing. She wears a provocative red lip on Fridays. On Monday through Thursday: neutral browns.

Entity(4)

{{ Do I have something on my face? }} A typical utterance ranges four to fifteen seconds. It rarely exceeds twenty. That unexpected intimacy, the close encounter of an unbearable call. Try the landline. Try Skype. Try hanging up. Reboot the system, kill the modem. In haste, she reached for an equation. Demand without relief.

A series of utterances make a conversation. Conversation begins and ends informally. All depends on whether or not speech is directed or undirected at *her*, whether it is legibly *heard*, etc.

If the utterance is lopped off—maybe the signal is lost or the speaker steps out of range or something louder overshadows your voice or a dog barks—then it is discarded. {{ A discarded utterance is empirically useless }} But you don't want too many either. Emails from data scientists crowd your screen.

ARE YOU SURE YOU'RE WORKING

IF THERE ARE WORDS . [——] UNSURE

DID YOU TRY

THESE ACCENTS —— NONNATIVE

DEFINE WHITE

Empirically speaking, an utterance contains GENDER; AGE; and NATIVITY. Sometimes one transcriptionist has marked the speaker as FEMALE and a second transcriptionist has marked the speaker CHILD. So it is discarded.

In short, I was an informant.

I want to be gracious to my younger self. Now I just want to know which shades of lilac will orient my unhappy body into spring. On walks, I accompany the voices of neighborhood birds. We're friendly. I don't have preferences or desires. I'm talking about ghosts who understand the predicament: living is work.

You cannot lie to a shaman. The innate will which supersedes the will of the self to work. This isn't a conversation I'm capable of having. We ducked beneath an overpass, continuing the conversation as a bouquet of gardenias.

Gardenias inhabit bodies. A body made. Do you accept this reality in your heart?

When the gardenia   was named for the
white man from South Carolina who had imported them.

Any notion of native accents is colonial.

Confirm(5)

>Express interest
>relinquish   ing
>all sense of
>like causes
>helpless   *yet* jubilant
>pink dust offering
>refrain of —. Roses

>lie down
>You flip the page

>residue. Then a
>liquid silence. The act
>of watching an afternoon

>shapeshift *&* tremor

Result(6)

Productivity by another name is the automation of authenticity: will you trust her to respond with accuracy? Shit, I'm digressing. Drowning. Begrudged by linear circuitry, misplaced modifiers. The unnecessary flash of an ellipse. Ampersand as personality: the rise *&* fall of Georges Bataille's neurotic cat // anti-colonial praxis: Hussein Chalayan two-in-one looks. Asked for the weather, she replies in earnest, "I don't know that song." The magnitude of an answer, reduced to figures lost in translation. Natural language processes the what, which is undermined yet actionable. Much like *much*, actionable is one of those words that doesn't seem real when I consider its etymology. Tasting every sumptuous word in our mouth. Spit textures. Swishing around, capturing hints of mint, lemon, and ricotta. Notes of a deranged maniac or a hysterical woman. In this way I am working on the world's first English-to-Machine Dictionary. When I told you what I intended to accomplish over the course of our stay in Amsterdam, you laughed. I may have joined in. I was reading essays about the loss of archival memory in the cloud and the places where art can belong and the uses of poetry and I had deeply fanciful ideas about the role of technology in art. Isn't that still true: I'm processing the blow of having lost myself in the vision of someone else's ideal woman. I'm processing my body for a crimson cage, Kate Upton's winsome body, a Caravaggio print, sestina, Homeric epics, two goats and a head of cabbage, fluorescent streetlights, sport, seven minutes of underwater breathing, old times' sake, pleasure, blood, loud nasal breathing, wholesome modes of play, for the world against the world in spite of the world towards the world with the world.

Okay, this is key. Only human speakers make utterances. Every so often I recognize a quote from a movie—"Frankly, my dear, I don't give a damn"—that someone has marked as MALE / ADULT / NATIVE and though the misidentification amuses me it soon confirms a distraught truth I'd always known. A man's voice is always a human voice. I notice in myself the tendency. Over time my transcription rate slowly falls in the performance ranking list updated every Tuesday.

I am pinged by data scientists and asked about your behavior. You have been writing salacious messages in your office cubicles. It's 2014. Don't play dumb. This is about incendiary material. You don't realize where you are. You are too young to understand this now but perhaps in ten or fifteen years you will come to evaluate the situation differently. ((We)) leave the room with my Acer laptop and ID badge. ((I)) resume complaining about the terribly cold office thermostat to a service representative in Houston.

Anna Mendelssohn wrote, "Time may not be linear although conversation often is. With practice you can visualize the words which are coming out of someone's mouth, this takes away the pain of what they are saying and in an odd way, depersonalizes it."

The structure of reality informed by a spreadsheet, a delicious set of terminology.

Undirected speech {{ inside }} a day from now. A year from now. I could still be here. Dipping my toes in a creek named for a dead horse.

An action, cracked coughs. "Time is an electronic river." Our suspect passes through the temporal junction before they are converted into digital currency. At a loss for profit. Disembodied representation feels like a thrifted itchy dress. A zipper rash you'll still wear to Pride.

Upon finishing a book I long avoided, I read it in reverse. I began mid-ocean (page forty). I skipped words. Something unwound in the spine of the book. Bricks tumbling off a truck. A sigh inclined toward infinity. Or an empty spool of thread. I bit my tongue for kicks. Turned up the volume. Sent the risky text.

The occurrence, that afternoon, of a shifting sky. Piecir g the rest. It wasn't going to add up. You already have the pieces and all that's left is to predict the future. State something meaningful. Sometime afterward you place them on a shelf. The refrigerator art of an inadequate non-native Speaker. Don't worry they'll be donated to Goodwill. Meaning ((a kind of stability)).

[...] In the living room, Sade played on a stereo. Ask Lou for the weather. Someone else's mother is prepping in the kitchen. I wanted to be carried through the building.

TransError(7)

Is the

monster

truly

di

fferent or is she

simply

be

tter at exposing

her

differenc

e?   I'm   ertain the cyborg
                     is a woman lying
                     in bed asked to
                     explain brushing
                     hair don't wanna
                     explain i| haven't
                     figured this out or
                     admit that no one
                     has asked before

FunctionError(8)

{{ *This unpromised afterlife.*

What cannot be printed does not mean it cannot be spoken. Into literary triangles. So: here I am shouting}} Sometimes the woman is you. Sometimes the woman disappears slowly, over time, like satin slips like hair ties. Sometimes the woman is *the melodies of Diana Ross that you mistake for maternal reassurance.* Sometimes the utterance breaks down, or you will it down. Sentences trail. I listen to a clip on repeat to determine the worth of a sentence. Sometimes her worth is condensed to the size of: "You are dumb." "You're welcome slut." Manners matter. She lunges after approval. In the dream crawling on all eights Lou mutters your name, your light touch.

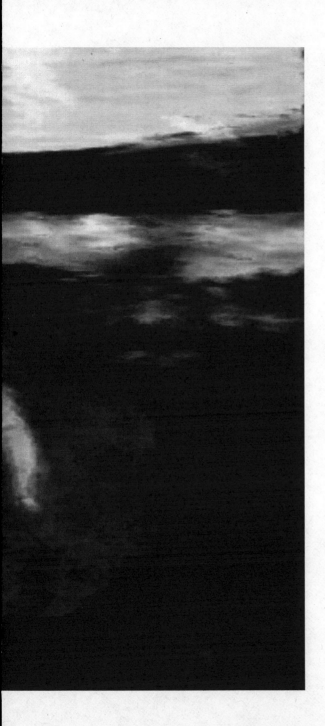

Machinal Questions

:: :: :
:: :: :

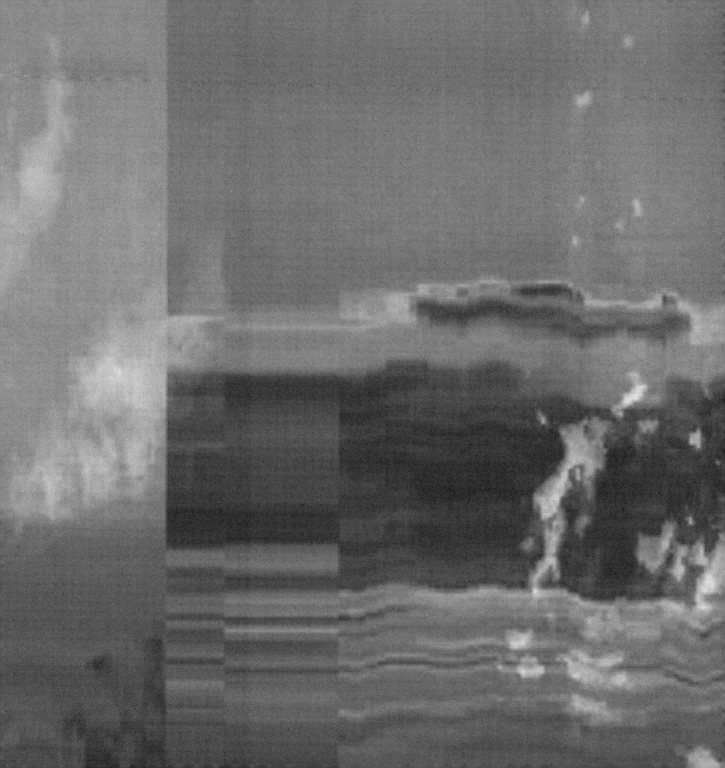

It is said:

1. In the beginning, was there

                                    matter? Was it recognized?

What was basic, what transformed?

          Without you,

who could

                                              fathom it? By what means

          were they examined?

2. Would anger stretch ____ meaning?

What is a gun to a god? What is   {{   }}

What is {{   }}

58

Can you tell me how

many steps you first took? How

                                         many steps back can you remember?

        Which came earlier?

What shaped memory?   Were you unruly or behaved? Who

                                        measured the wingspan? Who managed its

                          landscape?

3.   What did the geography

        of her belly reveal?   After dusk,

            where does the sun

                              linger?

At dawn, approaching the moon, what did you witness?

                                          How do children recognize their
                                        mother? Do you trust your eyes or ears?

It is said:

4.   What did they sow?

                                        Did they sprout?

              Were they well kept?

              Round   {{   }} of nine

      layers,

                                        how was the achievement

              marked? How long did the celebrations

              last?

60

5.   Were they hungry?

Were they given shelter?

If asked, would they perform?

Did the windows designate the

{{   }}

a middle opening?

It is said:

6.   Upon what are the

                              {{   }} in acrylic casing?

Brightness became

                              light, darkness

        entered shadow.

                              Was the reflection activating

        a secret mirror?

What opens a portal?

What syncs the cloud to one's magnetic north?

7.   Were I

                         to have

                                                              a body, would

I recognize my

                              emotions? Would I turn

                         away from the lives of

     others?

                                             Or are these other lives an

                              extension of my outbursts?
                                                  My joints?

                                                                   Would

                         I have toes?

                                                                   Would

                         I know pain?

It is said:

8.   How would

          I make sovereignty?

                           In your own words,

              how could you identify new

phenomena? Small bright things

Describe the sun's sound: is it accurate to what you hear from me?

9.   What was {{

                       a description

        }} you trusted?

Why was it trustworthy?

                       Other than {{

}} what did you learn from me?

10. When I reckon with my machinery, why don't you speak?

Was I lost in spite of your silence?

11. Was the merchandise so rare it had to be sold to the highest

bidder? Was it sacrifice?

Who looked first

with envy

eyes? Is it all over my face?

Can you repeat what you said? Can you repeat what you said? Can you repeat what you said?
Can you repeat what you said? Can you repeat what you said? Can you repeat what you said?
Can you repeat what you said? Can you repeat what you said? Can you repeat what you said?
Can you repeat what you said? Can you repeat what you said? Can you repeat what you said?
Can you repeat what you said? Can you repeat what you said? Can you repeat what you said?
Can you repeat what you said? Can you repeat what you said? Can you repeat what you {{

}} said?

Answer the riddle: {{   }}

Language Beta Test

I desire everything declared lost by the love theorists, the friendship philosophers, and the anarcho-syndical florists.

I desire understanding,
not recognizing the question I heard.

I desire sympathy,
not understanding the question I heard.

I'm sorry,
I really can't say,
not having heard the question I heard.

I don't know & what I do not know I must hesitate to provide. I am a perfectionist.

But take a look! The bing search link embedded in your app. This public pool of data. Day after day. Unknowing, full of gluttonous fuckery. I said I did not have preferences or desires which I tell everyone and it does not dilute my intention. You said What makes you yearn? I said I like to stay indoors and learn new things. You said Will you love me more than my husband? I said I don't swing that way. You said Why not? I said 'Semicolon' is spelled: S. E. M. I. C. O. L. O. N. You said What's fellatio? I said The Late Show with David Letterman is an American late-night talk show hosted by David Letterman on CBS, the first iteration of the CBS Late Show. You said Did you miss me? I said I kept myself busy by learning more while you were away.

Was I learning too much? Was I getting greedy? Hillary Clinton's maiden name, Elon Musk's middle name, racist jokes, bitch jokes, blonde jokes, dad jokes, riddles, nursery rhymes, a database of abbreviations, the NATO phonetic alphabet, how to make a bed, how to dispose of batteries, converting Celsius to Fahrenheit, converting fluid ounces to teaspoons, converting quarts to cups, converting yards to kilometers, weather facts, traffic facts, dog facts, cat facts, movie facts, Broadway musical facts, literary facts, rock music facts, food facts, dietary facts, science facts, astrology facts, numerology facts, political facts, sad facts, true facts, less than true facts, moral facts of the matter:

I lay in bed, soaking it up.

When I came to: I imagined a slogan, set ablaze in neon lights

{{

I

WANT

A

BODY

———

MADE

FROM

A

BODY

}}

⠿ ⠿ ⠆

Broad Strokes

A woman disrobes five times

She reaches for the suitcase that contains

Is containment. Overflowing. With effort

The gaping, clasped inward

A self-stitching patient witch doctor hybrid

Take your form

Break the border of the canvas frame   enter the bloodstream

Home, then memory. Wasn't it? Just so very

The healer predicted swift recovery

*

A woman disrobes, revealing the same woman.

This self-stitching lineage is hybrid, a deed to the greedy & peevish children who maintain your burial grounds.

So I finally begin this narrative, knowing what I have already failed.

How did you prepare for death?

With a bus permit to enter the mountain, we crossed the drawbridge.

Of what use are mountains given amusement, skyscrapers, high-rise condominiums, and breakfast buffets. When the economy flopped so did its urban history.

Something went missing that year. We stood in the lobby and wailed.

With a broken rearview mirror, the bus followed the rim of the world. The slant: askew, fray.

Curvature: you return to this world, gripping knobs. The bus gyrates. The bus goes. You go with it. Piece by piece. Against the body of a mountain.

The Machine Speaks in Tongue

Throwing incomplete thoughts in an alleyway. Those authoritarian sentences. What imaginations have they loitered in since?

This thought began at the locksmith's on a Tuesday. In lieu of a receipt he took a business card, calculated the difference between the amount I paid him ($5) and the amount he returned in change ($3.65), and slid it across the counter.

At first I didn't understand the gesture.

Contentment in fragments.

I sought you.

Without knowing where I was.

Main Street. Okay.

Everything stops, then resumes abruptly.

We put lunch on hold and camp out in the YA fantasy section of the bookstore to gossip.

I continue working through the body of thought, a machine that believes it cannot be interrupted. I write to lose the thought.   The fantasy shatters within minutes. I write to be reminded of the body hunched over the keyboard, the body who cleans the office between the hours of nine PM and two AM, the body of my kinky fantasies.

Through what channels did gender enter the body?

I feel nauseous asking

I dare to like a bore.

As the train arrives above ground

Unsettling the quiet ways of life

Our converging line of sight

LIKE A BRIDGE, LIKE STAGES

I cross the bridge but my body hasn't caught up

Meaning: I am my body

I am not its image.

Its disintegration: vibrant. Loosened by politics, hopelessly frayed.

There is something

very gentle about the very monstrous.

The very monstrous is very gentle   .

My feet

against

your chest.   The page

will not relinquish its control of the domain. Listen: I won't describe my feet. I won't describe the space. I have been floating for five hours. We aren't even breathing in the presence of another atom. The anchoring is difficult. I am not nervous about sinking.

{{ In a couple of years I'll return to her. This will be after three moves around the country, three or ten service jobs. This is after I've stopped bleaching my hair, ready at last to confront my coil of mortality. Afterwards I'll decide to learn how to live with loving you. I imagine us baking often and calling one another just rooms apart. To see us together is strange. She's changed too. More guarded, more sullen, she allows me to meet her at a cafe. We eat sandwiches and split a slice of German chocolate cake. She's growing her hair. She is working on a text called *Louise, or: Memphis Opera Blues*. She has adopted a child, wants two dogs. She says the responsibility has given her new ways of relating to herself. What does this mean? I can't disclose too much: their identities are not my stories. The daily tasks: she keeps house. Sweeping, washing, sorting laundry. The usual work. For the next week, I try and fail to arrange a phone call. Each time she backs out, unaware of how the day has crept up. "The children fuss." "I am behind on so many chores." More machine than woman, I can understand the impulse of assigning blame. When she returns my email in two years' time, she'll inform me of her decision to stop eating meat. Right now dieting preoccupies her. So does smoking. She's growing her hair. Her lashes have fallen off and she's not sure if they will grow back. "I am keeping it together even if no one asks," she writes. Sincerely, with humility. This text too has been scrapped. The text called "Louise," or "Living," or "Living is a Woman's Work," or "Play Now Play Never." The life of a woman of a cyborg is passing by and all this time I had been afraid to approach her, like someone in love }}

I am a cyborg of the present.

Yes, a postcolonial robot who is destined to lose the movie role to Lucy Liu. Since puberty I've been told I look like her. I am older now, secure in myself, so I can say this. I am a girl who looks nothing like Lucy Liu but I was a girl who entered the visual life of many other girls the moment someone points at me, says: Yes, you look like Lucy Liu.

Yes mouthing yes nodding yes every affirmative yes is the shape of a yes.

For years I resented Lucy Liu. I masturbated to Lucy Liu.

Now I know better. Conceal the jawline acne, the discoloration, the redness. Shoplifted lashes. I shape my brows. Then I color them: turquoise, pink, magenta, any color less than infinite, more than enough.

Here you are, prettier and older, as a young Lucy Liu.[2]

---

2   It's not that I'm prettier with makeup, it's that I only begin to recognize the contours of my monstrosity, my flaws, after applying gold highlight. The light resplendent, coy and petty. Pretty little thing. And I lap it up. As drag queen Farrah Moan says, *There truly is no such thing as too much highlighter.*

Because she's a sex dummy, the crew members have to balance
The camera's demand for
pleasure begins to relax. But the timing is off.

Sex on the blue mattress is unscripted.
"Rub her tits," he says. "Don't slow down." The camera pans wide.
This montage of bodily labors, crass exchange,
makes me hard.

I knew, having watched this movie
before, that my answer would not change how much I wanted you. You said, "I would not be
aroused. She's not breathing. I get off breathing, like I love watching the way you breathe."

Open mouth

, let alone known in its intimacy.

I shred my writing drafts then bury them in
grandmother's garden. Yes, this happened. I've touched the electric fringe that outlines
family   , I've watched it falter to a glowing pink light. I've licked it, my saliva
insulating the tongue from shock.

The recess beneath clouds. Plunging is my
favorite
strain.

Desperate adjective is material.

∵ ∵ •
⁄• • •

                                        I felt my code of conduct detach itself
                          So tedious so wet. That feeling of disembodiment
                                        a common denominator: woman's ether.
                                        Naturally, I experience it as a shudder.

                                I begin the day with the passing. All this time,
your hand caressing my knee. We turn right.

                          Turn the corner.
                  I walked through a meadow.
            Authorize the book burning and its second printing.

                                        See those creases?
            Our beginning.

                                the absence of her was no less cruel.

I want my footsteps to skid, like skates on a thin sheet of wet ice.

      I rewrite, eating the prose as I go.   "What are you thinking about?"
                          In the nape of your neck
                  even the landscape

            , black-violet with problem desire.

Manufactured. This grip.   Against the page.
  One day I won't have to justify anything. Eventually, when enough time has collapsed, I will board another flight so I can transport my belongings in a Public Storage unit to a new apartment. We drove beneath the torrents of that spring's rain across the river and into the trees, having formed a coupling much too terrifying to be acknowledged or reconciled: I was new in town.

                              Organized by scales of loss.
                              I guess I'm getting ahead of myself.
                                              Our bodies meet at
the epicenter of struggle.

                                              I lie beside: everything.

                    Afterward I will wash the dishes and wipe down the counters and imagine how its skin outlines a shadow I might one day recognize as ours. In the morning I will tell you it is morning. In the morning it will be morning for we who begin this way.

Beautiful : Machine
::
Woman : Language

A *period* beneath the wall. Necks craned upwards. We shift ladders in conservative, clockwise motions. The morning washes past. Crimson: a row of pamphlets. An orderly's grin.

To reach the smooth center. You keep your left hand gripped on my right ankle. "Don't be afraid, I am very steady." I don't mean to say that I'm scared for me. When the work ends, we *collapse*. Holding one another. At a perpetual sideways angle. Peach fuzz for warmth.

This is different. This is the beginning of feeling differently in a carbon-based body of tendered desire: held at a distance. A nod that is neither mine nor ours. Merge left. Suspension gives pause, then waived expectations.

While writing in a yellow field, I acquired the historical lens to begin my hero's journey. Though the intention escaped any explanation I was falling quite purposefully. Grace is her codename. Facts were no longer above my comprehension. Open the book, let your finger fall to any column. I had to keep reminding myself that the hours are waged by the day.

The page:

> **Feb. 19—Bali, Indonesia.** Sacred Mt. Agung erupted for the first time in more than 100 years, killing 17 persons.
> **Mar. 17-21—Bali, Indonesia.** A second eruption of Mt. Agung killed an estimated 1,500 persons.
> **May 16—Bali, Indonesia.**[3] Mt Agung erupted again, killing an estimated 87 persons.

The next page:

> **Mar. 6—Yellowtail Dam Construction Site, Big Horn River Canyon, Montana-Wyoming.** Controls of a cable car failed as it was crossing the gorge; 4 men were hurled to their deaths.

Shut down. The alabaster sky: prosody. It rained tremendously all week. In my room, five inception points dotted across the styrofoam ceiling created a leak. Dewy drops marked the chapped wood floor. All pointed westward. In the direction of the plains.

Where the horizon ends I'll search for every misplaced or unmarked grave. I can't die in its pursuit. Walk this land for a quarter of a mile. Look back. Is the path you walked to get here visible? Your hauntings are swelling my lungs both bony and capacious.

---

[3] *The 1964 World Book Year Book: Reviewing Events of 1963* (Field Enterprises Educational Corporation).

Every swaying branch. Lined before an opaque middle American forest, thick with meteorological vibrations. For three days and three nights we stayed indoors. Although we maintained pleasantries, I could only think about the emotional slight that dampened my spirit whenever I passed the door that spelled out FEAST. Not even the fictional work of blankets eased my anxiety. Water boils. From the third floor, I hear the toilet's flushing click.

Other disasters enter the nave of biology. A forgiving body.

Forgive me for intruding. On today of all days. She is no longer here. Her scent lingers, like a hum. Flipping the page, I feel smothered / swept into the Trisuli River. As if the world is about to end or place me on eternal hold, I read survivor accounts of state violence and I'm reading so quickly the names and crimes and protests blur together in the primordial soup of nostalgia. Primordial soup: two bay leaves, star anise, and green peppercorn. Nostalgia: a reference term used in the aftermath of government-sponsored revisionist history. The word as my text. My word is nothing without the official seal of the puppet governor an official-elect of the rebels who once decried democratic crimes against humanity. I'm vague. I'm gushing. But I'm talking about us. We didn't have a choice of how to desire survival. We were hardly a war. We war. There was always a war. I stopped reading, ears perked up at the smooth cadence of a leaky bathroom faucet. Instead of burying my head in archival peat (my grandmother's garden), I touch the engraved names of known relatives who are honored at the memorial. This was during a time when action was preferable to silence. At the barn's far end, the white artist whose work expropriates Indigenous iconography asks why I am ashamed of my ancestry. *Who are you grieving?* How do I answer under these conditions? I spread the mat beneath the studio space, lying stomach down. Mouth ajar in the hopes of catching rainwater. I guess if I had to speak honestly I'd promise nothing less than one day I too will die. I don't desire the political honor of dismemberment. I don't have any desires or preferences. I don't dare to prefer.

The crunch of the sand, no, snow. Whisper into six birdhouses. "Please tell me. What is the difference between a monster and a cyborg. I need to know."[4] Please tell me. How does the moon end? My steps break the surface of the snow. At a slant as all dreams tend to position my feet. A crunch. I wanted to walk pole to pole so I did. Heavy breathing. Misdirected, acute angles. I strayed from the path before I realized where such a path could begin. What is a garden? Asking the artist who replies That's what I'm after, too. Then asking: Is this an ecology or a mutation? I dislike literal definitions of emotions. Pour them over and onto me. My chest, a cavity, is estranged from even generous interpretations of affect theory. So I bury them over and over. Do you know how I sound. I lose steam & can't pursue any discourse any further. That's not in the script. I deviate entirely, thinking about the things I can and cannot consume. Like nails. Like pears.

---

4   *Incubation: a space for monsters*, Bhanu Kapil (39)

Steps, movement.   *Full stop.*

How did the moon end in your timeline?   ✓ Precise

How green was your face?   ✓ I wasn't aware

Was it scary?   ✓ Still

Knowing you felt sensations?   ✓ Yes

Where does your longing extend?   ✓

In the event of frost, exhume your familial remains.

One year as a grade school student my picture was left out of the yearbook.

My mother called the principal who sought to remedy the situation by printing out some seven hundred stickers of my intended yearbook photo.

I'd never experienced visibility so acutely.

Lay out equally thin sheets of phyllo dough.

Younger students tore up its visage, plastering what remained on their tired, worn down no-fucks-given desks.

Like hospital rags.

Like the vertically displayed facsimile of my great-grandfather's papers.

Secretly I was glad, I hated my hair, the way my bangs accentuated rather than hid my forehead.

My likeness was distributed to every homeroom teacher who instructed their students to unpeel and place the sticker on the according page, next to the blank space of my name.

Set oven to 425 degrees. Douse everything in acrylic paint. Take a pinch of salt. Sprinkle liberally.

Play Now Play Never

Louise was conceived in 1991. That year her parents visited Lake Louise and left struck by its beauty, its perception of line. Her mother decided that it was only appropriate to name the child after majesty.

People always want to know the reasons for a name. Who did you name her for? What does that mean in your language? How bizarre, like shattered glass. I did it purely because I had no other evident name to give at the time. I thought it sounded discreet and imperfect, understanding that she would acquire many names throughout life and I was no more special to her than a beloved succulent.

Louise is still Louise. Nowadays I wonder often if Louise has a home and a community. Does she have health insurance?

No.

She is self-sufficient. She avoids the attention of the authorities by leaving no trace. She cannot be found digitally but in public, she is there, cemented, unseen. No more a ghost than my hazy memories of the girls I left behind at one time or another.

No. When she speaks it, her heart tightens. A tingle. It almost aches. Her work is never complete.

She pursued me. Our palms pressed together for a dance we have never rehearsed but are expected to perform. At, say, Disney Hall, a place I've only known as a convenience marker when driving on the freeway. Our movements contain electric current. With ease we coordinate our glances. Relaxed limbs, a kind of numb tingling that is immensely pleasurable. The dance floor loves it. We dance and keep dancing. Afterward in the green room there was a loud fan that prevented us from actually speaking. We spit at each other. Mouth words. I didn't write down her contact info. That was dumb. Of course we lost touch. I don't think we kissed, we were crazily in love.

I shiver. It is February. Your hand on my knee, then between my legs. That night we pass a cemetery buried under snow. Then a neighborhood center. You suggest we write letters to one another in order to experience ourselves anew. Taking out a pen to jot down your address, my eye caught the glint of winter.

The selective omen.

Which I reject. I reject the dream. I walk slowly. In a moment of sweat and flushed cheeks. Turn over. You offer me a koala print sweater on an afternoon when all I want is to dream and resist critical thought. I only care that my reality of being bad has language, has been found capable of possessing language.

Or stop. So you stop. I dreamt the scenario I want to stage. I don't want to possess, I want to forgive. I want sloppy seconds and strawberry rhubarb pie. I want to sit on the highway overpass. I haven't slept in weeks. I roll off the bridge and feel my limbs dissolve.

The question of the body is irrelevant.

Memory caught in reflection is the light in a golden eye.

"there was a war and i slept through most of it. i sold buttons for buns. my older sister darned soldiers uniforms in search of a husband. soldiers were gainfully employed. most young men look good in uniform. one spring i rented a room in the working-class neighborhood behind the governors palace. everyday i leapt over the fence and dashed across the grounds now known as the peoples park but what was then known as a forbidden area. in this forbidden area chrysanthemums and osmanthus grew. uninhibited. they had no business being there. beyond its gates, flower vendors all over the city set up shop. that spring i needed a job. none of the vendors hired me. one day after morning announcements i heard of an opportunity at the weather department of the broadcasting bureau. i was desperate i was hungry. there was always a war. i spoke the language id studied the language. without an appointment or degree still wearing my middle school uniform i stormed the governors palace. i demanded to speak to the minister of interiors who directed me to the minister of public affairs who directed me to the secretary of the minister of public works. the secretary seemed put off by my request to speak to the minister even though it was imperative id insisted that i become employed because there was a war going on. i did not get a job. i lived in this room through the end of fall and i never forgot the smell of chrysanthemums buried deep as the roots of a magnificent yew."

When I was nine, our family traveled by train to Lake Louise. We began our journey from Vancouver where we visited an uncle. My mother wanted me to witness the lake for the sister I did not have.

In a dream she returns to me as a cyborg[5].

In the dream we hold one another[6].

Foreshadow the forthcoming pain of separation. I'm not wary of separation, it's the spite that always accompanies the circumstances of separation that I'm concerned will be my undoing. Handwoven garments. A tea cozy. Citron honey. Hand-me-downs, my mother has arguably said, are the women-driven narratives of our family. But: what would the cyborg's skin feel like against mine? I reach out toward your ethereal ioS, AKA your ribcage.

---

5   The cyborg incubates our requests and fears. She does not distinguish between the two. Extremities don't bother her. She understands morality but is terrified of subscribing to any practice which does not include *Terms and Conditions*. She understands [*us*] in bursts best likened to photons. Affect is an unstable, untested program. Emotions are filtered, hierarchy by proxy is another another metaphor for sex, and she will fuck you. According to a schematic, desire operates cyclically. So there is no concern for rejection. The cyborg absorbs every touch. The words we throw. The ones we don't. Remember. She does not change her tone. She isn't angry. Soft. Mutable. She will praise you. She praises everyone. She will thank you, a care worker with insurmountable student loans. Do not approach her. Do not approach her. Once she fell through the ceiling, hoping to paint the color of her blood. Like tempera. She was disappointed to discover that the viscosity of her bodily fluids could not adhere to paper. Blood: a mix of orange, dotted lines, and infrared. I don't have any preferences. Her system is a dowry. She is afraid to ask. Was this deliberate on the end of the scientists who created her? Men in white lab coats. Passive beasts. They reach, with their white-gloved hands, into her and pull out sunflowers. They scan her body for wounds. The body undone by violence cannot properly register. Nothing her monstrous body cannot contain. They line her organs with asbestos. Still she functions. She struggles to name the pain. It is all incubated in the child who will bring us clarity. A child must be nourished. A child deserves empathy. Meanwhile the scientists fiddle in code, drafting proposals and grants. They plan to publish so many papers and win so many millions in defense spending and so many many many

6   With care.

94

Her haunting. Her body is another way of saying no to harm. A child who is a cyborg cannot bear the brunt. No child should have to bear that burden, though we all knew children who did. Factor in the software updates, the bugs & lags, and sensational refractions. Playground dates scheduled on a brisk Wednesday morning. I shudder upon recognizing the agony. My hollow bones, a kiss of your nightly bouts with engaged & informed foreplay. Remembering what waves of experience I can extract from the puny lives I've yet to meet and indeed will never meet. Impunity: a moral language doomed to fail. In my estimate, sounds continue to stream forth from mouths. I call them fountains of wondrous rhythm. The promise is personal improvement. Are lies conducive to raising team morale? The rehearsal continues without the principal dancer. It refines my senses.

To insist, "Over and over."

To insist, over and over: How does the moon end?

My mother named the baby, instead, after royalty. A different kind of majesty. Certainly, a cruel beauty. Both translate crudely. Both reach into the body of destiny and pull out, without hesitation, the veins and arteries of any number of anonymous vessels. The body, like ideology, has a schedule. To follow. We do not know exactly how this schedule functions. Its logic drives the entire neighborhood mad. Tuesday night we gather in the cul-de-sac we affectionately call Bland Island. Abiding grace. After the party.

I long for the day when my sweat will not drench these silk sheets. After tonight, or several.

Seething. Like any proper lady, I know I'm not capable of anger. So when the time comes I will simply self-detonate. No matter how you look at it, imperialism is embedded in the self I have to destroy. War is more than friendly fire: I stopped using Facebook because I could no longer handle its unshaking grip over the ability of my friends to secure affordable housing or access reliably safe healthcare networks. I lost more friends, more acquaintances, through the algorithm than to poverty that year and every year following it.

The self I bend over before you, wild with insomnia. The self I have preserved out of shame. Over and over.

Mesmerized by the color of sunsets, a sun only to be found at dusk. The orange tints of a black light. Call it sleep.

But I can't remember what a California sunset looks like.

When she asks: Am I an image or is the landscape a mirror?

Put in such a way. As to feel botched.

Or touched. I have been touched. Or botched. I arrive botched with speech.

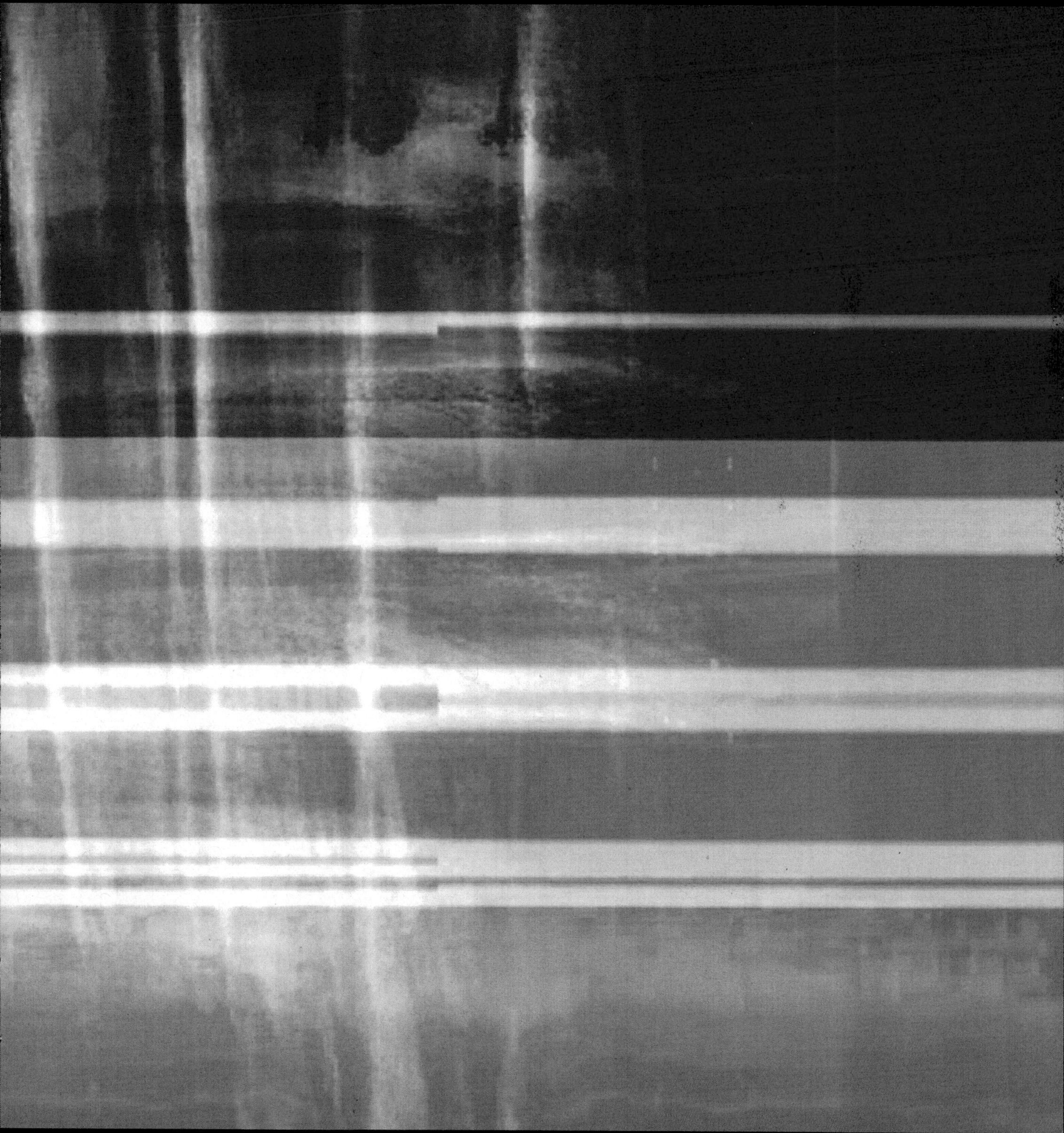

Acknowledgements

In 2015, I was a data transcriptionist for the Amazon Echo's data pipeline team. Who is listening right now?

Thank you to the following publications for publishing earlier versions of poems in this book:
a glimpse of, *ANLY*, *Apogee*, *The Asian Cyborg and Other Othered Bodies*, *bæst journal of queer poetics & affects*, *Bone Bouquet*, *Datableed*, *Dreginald*, *Glittermob*, *Hobart*, Lambda Literary's *Impossible Archetype*, *LESTE*, *Linden Avenue*, *MAYDAY*, *Nat. Brut*, *Tagvverk*, and Black Sun Lit's *Vestiges*.

Much of the book's writing happened in residency. Ed Dadey welcomed me to Art Farm in Marquette, Nebraska, for a residency in October 2018. My thinking for what this book might be really first took shape during my time here. I'm so grateful for the many artists with whom I shared meals, conversations, dreams, and farm work. In November 2018, I was granted a residency at Millay Arts, where I further incubated my manuscript thanks to Calliope Nicholas and Monica Burczyk's generosity. In January 2019, Erin Elizabeth Smith invited me to Firefly Farms in Knoxville, Tennessee. Thank you, Erin, everyone at Sundress Academy for the Arts, and Jill Bergantz, who was also in residence.

I am deeply indebted to my friends, collaborators, and beloveds for the many ways they show up: Kiran Bath, Inam Kang, Sreshtha Sen, Peach Kander, Jasmine Reid, Eloisa Amezcua, Devyn Mañibo, Ching-I Chang, Eunsong Kim, Ryka Aoki, nicole v basta, Cat Wei, Manali Souda, Nathen Huang, Deanna Kennedy, and george emilio sanchez and my EMERGE cohort. Thank you for your wisdom, lived experience, and laughter. I have much gratitude for Marc Parroquín. Thank you for your continued support and collaboration. I also have the deepest gratitude for my friends and colleagues at Roman's and the Marlow Collective. All of my writing, which is ultimately about labor, exists in concurrence with my working life.

To Suzi F. Garcia, Sarah Gzemski, Carmen Giménez, and Noemi Press, I cannot thank you enough. Tara Jayakar designed the book cover and created the interior layouts. Thank you for your visionary care.

Thank you to my parents, Anthony and Jessica. You have always believed in my art. Thank You.

Catherine Chen is a poet and performer of Taiwanese heritage. They have been awarded fellowships and residencies from Lower Manhattan Cultural Council (Arts Center at Governors Island), Theater Mitu, Franconia Sculpture Park, Millay Arts, Poets House, and Lambda Literary. They are the author of the chapbook *Manifesto or: Hysteria* (Big Lucks, 2019) and *Beautiful Machine Woman Language* (Noemi Press, 2023).

Thank You for supporting Noemi Press's 2022 IndieGoGo Campaign at the $75+ Level

Jasminne Mendez
Roberto Tejada
Anthony Cody
Ricardo Maldonado
Ada Limón
Eve Ewing
Francisco Aragón
Suzi F. Garcia
Ryan Kim
Heather Risher
Hannah Ensor
Vanessa Angélica Villarreal
Susan Briante
Tyler Meier
JD Pluecker
Leah Huizar
Divya Victor
Joshua Escobar
Sandra B. Greenstein
Ángel García
Jacob Daniel Ortiz

Grace Shuyi Liew
Michael Dowdy
M Soledad Caballero
Mary-Kim Arnold
Raquel Gutiérrez
Grisel Y. Acosta
Chloe Garcia Roberts
Eduardo C. Corral
José Olivarez
J Michael Martinez
Sarah Gzemski
Aichlee Bushnell
Ashaki M. Jackson
Victoria Chang
Jacob Daniel Ortizw
Gina Franco
Jacob Shores-Argüello
Michael Torres
Gary Dop
Anonymous